Oops, Your Manners Are Showing™

A Study Course for Ages 8 & Up
Third Edition

Peggy Norwood & Jan Stabler

Student Workbook

Oops, Your Manners Are Showing
A Study Course for Ages 8 & Up
Student Workbook
Third Edition, 1999

Peggy Norwood & Jan Stabler
Copyright © 1994, 1995, 1996, 1997, 1999 by The Oops Group, Inc.

Scripture taken from
the KING JAMES VERSION.

the HOLY BIBLE, NEW INTERNATIONAL VERSION. Copyright © 1973, 1978,1984 International Bible Society. Used by permission of Zondervan Bible Publishers.

Published by
The Oops Group, Inc.
P. O. Box 5868
Katy, TX 77491

Houston area 281-347-1244
Toll Free 1-888-749-6677
Fax 281-347-1277
www.oopsgroup.com

Illustrated by Andrea Barth and Tera Yoshimura

Printed in the United States of America

ISBN 0-9660287-0-8

Other resources in the *Oops* series:
Oops, Your Manners Are Showing, A Study Course for Ages 8 & Up
    Teacher's Edition
Bible Search for Manners, Thirteen Lessons for Ages 8 & Up
Oops, Your Manners Are Showing, Lessons for Ages 4 to 7
    Teacher's Guide
Children Learn Manners as They Color
    Color Sheets
Manners Can Be Fun
    Song and Performance Soundtrack on Cassette

Oops, Your manners are showing! That's right, whether they are good or bad, your manners are always showing. After all, manners are how you say and do everything.

Are you ever in a situation where you do not know what to say or do? By practicing good manners, you can build your confidence and at the same time help others feel more comfortable.

Have you always thought that practicing good manners is only for special occasions? Every day of your life is special, and you often have the opportunity to help others feel special.

Certainly everyone can learn to use good manners. Showing consideration for others can become a natural way of life.

Table of Contents

Cast of Characters

Oopsman Family
Mamaw Nina Oopsman
Maddie and Mark Oopsman
Wilhelminanina Oopsman (Oops)
Paul Lite
Bow Wow the Dog

Neighbors
Rose and Moses Valentine

Friends
Joy Givens
Minnie Frenz
Eddie Kit
Hank Yu
Rudy Loudman

Hamilton Family
Heloise and Harold Hamilton
Alexandria Hamilton

Professionals
Governor Powers
The Reverend Divine
Dr. Spleen
Coach Freestyle
Mrs. Stagemaster

Courtesy Begins at Home

WELCOME

Proverbs 20:11

Even a child is known by his doings, whether his work be pure, and whether it be right.

King James Version

Even a child is known by his actions, by whether his conduct is pure and right.

New International Version

Courtesy Begins at Home

The most important place to begin using good manners is at home with your family. The people closest to you should receive the greatest love, respect, and consideration. As you learn to please one another at home, you will be more successful in all your relationships.

1. Be considerate of others by accepting responsibility for personal grooming. Keep your hands and fingernails clean. Trim your nails evenly. Shampoo your hair; brush your teeth; bathe regularly; and use anti-perspirant, if needed. Wear clothes that are clean and neatly pressed.
   Examples:

2. Keep your room clean and neatly organized. Do your chores cheerfully and promptly; follow through with your parents' requests. Help your brothers and sisters with their chores.
   Examples:

3. Respect the privacy of others. Knock before entering someone else's room. Do not go through others' belongings or use personal items without asking for permission.
   Examples:

4. Be willing to share your time, your abilities, your belongings.
   Examples:

5.   Take care of borrowed items and return them promptly. If you have time to
      borrow them, you have time to return them.
      Examples:

6.   Accept responsibility for what you use. Clean up after yourself and put trash in its
      place. If you use the last paper towel, replace the roll. If you take out a board
      game, put it back in the proper place after you finish playing.
      Examples:

7.   Consider the needs of others. Offer a kind word, a friendly smile, and a helping
      hand.
      Examples:

8.   O_____ the shortcomings of others. Do you know it is bad manners
      to point out someone else's bad manners? In fact, someone else's bad manners do
      not excuse yours. You might say, "This is what I learned in Manners Class," and
      then let your family see you setting the example of good manners.

Introductions

Luke 6:31

And as ye would that men should do to you, do ye also to them likewise. King James Version

Do to others as you would have them do to you. New International Version

 # Introductions

Introductions can help people feel included and comfortable in meeting new friends. However, introductions can be awkward when you are trying to remember whose name to say first or what to say after you have introduced someone. While it is more important to make the introduction than it is to make it exactly right, introductions are easier if you know a few rules.

BEING INTRODUCED

1. Stand.

2. Look directly at the person and make eye contact.

3. Smile.

4. Give a brief, reasonably firm **h**_____.
   If someone extends her hand for a handshake, accept it.

5. Say hello and the person's name. "Hello, Mrs. Valentine, " "How are you (How do you do), Mrs. Valentine?" or "I'm pleased to meet you (It's nice to meet you), Mrs. Valentine."

INTRODUCING YOURSELF

1. Show you are interested in knowing someone by introducing yourself.

2. Say, "Hello, I'm _____."

3. If you have previously met the person but do not remember her name, it is best to reintroduce yourself.

4. Reintroduce yourself if you see someone you have met but perceive he does not remember you. (Do not ask the person if he remembers meeting you.)

5. There may be occasions when you need to say, "I'm sorry; could you tell me your name again?"

INTRODUCING OTHERS

1. Include last names

- ◆Use Mr. or Mrs. when introducing a child to an adult. Children should not use the first name of an adult without permission. "Rose, I'd like you to meet my daughter, Wilhelminanina. Her friends call her Oops. Oops, this is Mrs. Valentine."
- ◆When you introduce family members with your same last name, do not include last names. Include the last name of a family member if it is different from yours. Be sensitive if stepchildren are involved.

2. Whose name should you say first?

- ◆*non-family member*
  "Mrs. Hamilton, I'd like you to meet my mom and dad."
  Example:

- ◆ *VIP* ("Very Important Person" refers to someone in a very important position.)
  "Reverend Divine, have you met my drama teacher, Mrs. Stagemaster?"
  "Governor Powers, may I introduce Dr. Spleen?"
  Example:

- ◆*older person* ("Respect your elders!")
  Oops: Mamaw, this is my friend, Alexandria Hamilton. Alexandria, I'd like you to meet my Mamaw Oopsman.

  Alexandria: Hello, Mrs. Oopsman. It's nice to meet you.

  Mamaw: Thank you, dear, but please call me "Mamaw." Everyone does.
  Example:

- ◆*female* ("Ladies first!")
  "Alexandria, this is my cousin Paul Lite. Paul, Alexandria Hamilton."
  Example:

~ Introductions ~

3.   Do not repeat full names unless they are difficult. Do not say, "Alexandria Hamilton, this is Paul Lite. Paul Lite, this is Alexandria Hamilton."

4.   Be sensitive when introducing someone as your "friend." It may sound as though you are suggesting the other person is not your friend.

5.   If you forget someone's name, introduce the person whose name you know. Hopefully the other person will introduce himself. "Oh, have you met Alexandria Hamilton?"

6.   After the introduction, help initiate conversation by providing brief information about how you met the person you are introducing or about something that those involved have in common.

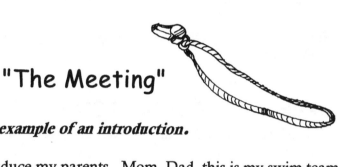

"The Meeting"

The following skit is an example of an introduction.

Oops: Coach, I'd like to introduce my parents. Mom, Dad, this is my swim team coach, Coach Freestyle.

Coach: *(Extending hand to Mark Oopsman)* It's good to meet you, Mr. and Mrs. Oopsman.

Mark: *(Shaking hands)* I'm glad to meet you, Coach Freestyle. Please call me Mark. Thank you for coaching the team.

Maddie: *(Extending hand to shake)* Hello Coach, I'm Maddie. Yes, thank you so much; Oops really enjoys the swim team.

Coach: You're very welcome. *(Looking at Oops)* I'm glad you're with us this year, Oops.

Oops: Oh thank you, Coach, and I'm glad you got to meet before the meet . . . I mean we met before the meet . . . I mean YOU met before the meet . . . I mean . . . see you at the meet.

INTRODUCTIONS IN A GROUP

1. Review your guest list right before your party. A last minute check will help you remember names and for whom to look as guests arrive.

2. When guests begin arriving, stay by the door and give a warm greeting. "Hello, it's nice to see you. I'm glad you could come."

3. Introduce arriving guests to those nearby. Call the names of those in a group to get their attention. "Paul Lite, Hank Yu, Eddie Kit, Joy Givens, and Minnie Frenz, I'd like you to meet Alexandria Hamilton."

4. Some guests may arrive later in the evening. As the host, stand and greet them.

5. If someone is leaving, it is not necessary to introduce him to guests who are entering.

INCORRECT INTRODUCTIONS

We all make mistakes, and introductions are no exception.

1. If you have just been introduced and your name has been given incorrectly, make the correction. "I know it's confusing, but my name is Oops, not Ouch."

2. If you begin incorrectly by saying the wrong name first, use the expression, "I'd like to introduce you to . . ."

    ♦ "Hank, I'd like to introduce you to Joy Givens." In this situation you are still giving honor to Joy.
    ♦ "Eddie, I'd like to introduce you to Alexandria Hamilton and Minnie Frenz." Using this introduction is less awkward than saying two or more names first.

INTRODUCING THE UNKNOWN GUEST

If you invite a friend to accompany you to a party or some other function, it is your responsibility to introduce him to others when you arrive. Do your best to help your friend feel part of the group.

It is important to **f**_____ on the person being introduced. Give

him your **f**_____ attention. When the person you have met walks away,

will he **f**_____ you were really glad that you met?

Crossword Puzzle

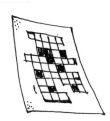

DOWN

1.   Introduce friends __ __ they enter a party.

2.   Mind your __ __ __ __ __ __ __.

3.   Another word for all right. __. __.

4.   __ __ introduce yourself if you think someone may not remember you.

5.   Talk about this cable station when you share an interest in sports. __ __ __ __

6.   __ __ __ __ when a guest enters your house or room for the first time. (Stand up)

8.   Extend this for a shake. __ __ __ __

13. Always consider the __ __ __ __ __ person.

14. Abbreviation for Identification. __ __.

16. Say, "It's so __ __ __ __ to meet you."

17. When you see Coach Freestyle, introduce your parents to __ __ __.

18. " __ __ __ do you do?"

19. Introduce men to __ __ __ __ __.

21. Fill in the blanks. Intro __ __ __ __

22. Politely introduce one person __ __ another.

23. Include __ __ __ __ names in introductions. (Opposite of first)

26. Two fishermen who meet may talk about a rod and a __ __ __ __.

27. __ __ __' __ forget to introduce your guests.

29. When meeting Alexandria Hamilton, __ __ __, "Hello, Alexandria."

30. Stand, look __ __ the person, and give eye contact.

31. Say you are glad you __ __ __ the person introduced.

21

~ Introductions ~

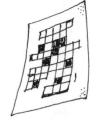

ACROSS

2. It is __ __ __ __ important to make the introduction than it is to make it exactly right. (opposite of less)

7. Mamaw __ __ __ __ __ __ hands with Oops's friends when Oops introduces them to her.

9. A child is introduced to __ __ adult.

10. Announce (This is a free answer, just fill it in.)

11. __ __ termine whose name you will say first in an introduction (non-family member, VIP, older person, or woman).

12. Int __ __ duce younger to older.

14. When Alexandria's dad introduces himself, he says, "Hello, __' __ Harold Hamilton."

15. When guests arrive, always __ __ __ __ __ and greet them. (opposite of sit)

19. __ __ help initiate conversation after an introduction. (A word for "us")

20. A __ __ __ __ __ __ should not use the first name of an adult without permission.

22. Use the rules of introduction as a __ __ __ __ to help build relationships.

24. Introduce others to government __ __ church officials.

25. You should give this kind of greeting (opposite of cool). __ __ __ __ __

28. If you __ __ __ that someone has not been introduced, introduce her.
(A word for "look")

29. If a family member's name is not the __ __ __ __ as yours, include the full name in the introduction. (opposite of different)

32. In our lives we __ __ __ __ __ need to make introductions.
(opposite of seldom)

33. Stand instead of staying __ __ __ __ __ __ when you are being introduced.

34. When your name is given __ __correctly, make the correction.

~ Introductions ~

Conversation

Ephesians 4:29

Let no corrupt communication proceed out of your mouth, but that which is good to the use of edifying, that it may minister grace unto the hearers.

King James Version

Do not let any unwholesome talk come out of your mouths, but only what is helpful for building others up according to their needs, that it may benefit those who listen.

New International Version

  # Conversation

A conversation can be an enjoyable experience. Let's look at some ways to help communicate and get to know people through conversation.

♦ Think before you speak.
♦ Always remember to show interest in others.
♦ Balance the conversation: give and take; talk and listen.
♦ Do not be afraid that you will not know what to say.

WHAT TO SAY AND HOW TO ACT

1. Approach the conversation cheerfully. Do not dwell on negative subjects. Have a good sense of humor. Be able to laugh at yourself.

2. Make direct eye contact and listen carefully. Allow the person the opportunity to finish what he has to say before changing the subject or directing the conversation to yourself.

3. Do not allow yourself to be distracted. Avoid distracting others with unnecessary noises or annoying habits.
   Examples:

4. Be aware of body language. Notice facial expressions or gestures that show anger, disagreement, sadness, and disinterest.

5. Ask polite questions to learn more about the other person. Examples: Ask about hobbies, favorite sport or school subject, church, family, and/or where he lives; ask parents and siblings about their day; ask parents and grandparents about their memories.

6. When answering questions, offer information that helps others learn more about you.

7. Talk about subjects that are of interest to everyone involved.

8. You do not have to be a "brain," but it is good to be informed about current events.

9. Strive to speak clearly and correctly. Avoid sounds like "uh huh," "uh uh," and "naaa."

10. Please say "Please," "Thank you," and "No, thank you." These words express respect and appreciation.

11. Sincere compliments are appreciated by almost everyone. Look for opportunities to compliment someone's new hairstyle, new clothes, and accomplishments. Graciously accept compliments without showing embarrassment.

12. Everyone has opinions and ideas, and many may be different from yours. It is important to consider thoughtfully what others have to say.

   ◆Try to see things from others' point of view. "I can see **y**_____ side of that."
   ◆Others may have good ideas. Try to make the most of them. God sends different ideas through different people. Thank them for the suggestions. Consider the suggestions. Decide if you can use the idea.

13. Laughing out loud and having a good time with your friends can be fun. Consider, however, that there may be times when this behavior is inappropriate or inconsiderate.

WHEN TO GREET

1. When you see someone you know, give a friendly hello and include her name. When greeting a person you have not seen in a long time, ask how she has been doing. Ask about her family, mutual friends, etc. Say it is nice to see her.

2. When passing someone you do not know, a nod or a hello is appropriate. Everyone is worthy of respect. (Be sure this is a safe situation.)

3. When you see the parent of a friend, greet her and ask about your friend.

4. If you are with your parents and meet a friend of theirs, say "Hello" and "Goodbye."

5. When a friend approaches as you are talking with someone, include the friend in the conversation.

6. If someone you know passes your table at a restaurant, greet him; introduce him if he does not seem to be rushed. If you stop to speak to friends, your conversation should be brief to avoid blocking the aisle and delaying their meal.

7. If someone you know comes in after the beginning of a meeting, church service, theater performance, or movie, wait until the event has ended before visiting.

8. When meeting someone's household staff, speak to them, but limit your conversation. Let them go about their work.

9. When a friend of your parents or another adult visitor comes to your home, stand and say hello. Introduce yourself if you are unacquainted. Return to what you were doing, but stand and say goodbye as the person leaves.

SAY, "EXCUSE ME," WHEN . . .

1. Sneezing and yawning. Cover your mouth and turn your head.

2. Not hearing or understanding a statement or question.
Instead of saying "huh" or "what," say . . .

   ◆"Excuse me, I didn't hear."
   ◆"I'm sorry, I didn't understand."

3. Walking in front of someone or passing between two people.
Try to walk behind them.

4. Interrupting a conversation.

   ◆Only interrupt when necessary.
   ◆Wait until the conversation is finished or come back later.

5. Bumping into someone. Remember to be considerate of others when passing through crowds.

   ◆Pay attention to those around you.
   ◆Keep a moderate, smooth stride. Be careful not to overswing your arms.

6. Belching. When someone else belches, j_____

   i_____ i_____ .

WHAT NOT TO SAY

Knowing what not to say can be as important in showing respect to others as knowing the right thing to say.

1. Avoid statements or questions that would hurt, offend, or embarrass others. Do not call names or in any other way draw negative attention to anyone.
Examples: anyone who is slow, overweight, very thin, or has special needs

   - Be cautious when making references to a person's finances, weight, or personal appearance. Do not ask personal questions, such as, how much something cost.
   - Be protective of those in need. Ask how you can help.
   - If you offend someone, tell the person you are sorry and ask for forgiveness.
   - If someone offends you, be willing to forgive and forget. We all make mistakes and can be insensitive at moments. Consider if there is some truth to the comments. Is there a lesson for you even though the comments could have been said in a kinder way?

2. Do not spread gossip or repeat anything sensitive. No matter how so-called interesting the gossip may seem, it is not worth the damage or pain it could cause by your repeating it. Even if no one told you not to repeat it and even if everybody knows it, do not be the one to keep it going.

3. When someone has told you something in confidence, do not share it with anyone. (You may need to share concerns with your parents.) Be cautious about sharing your secrets with others. If someone continues to ask you personal questions you would rather not answer, say politely, "I'd rather not talk about it, if you don't mind." The person should say, "No, of course not" and change the subject.

4. Do not whisper secrets in front of others or point your finger at people.

5. Do not tell untruths. In conversation, you are not just passing words back and forth; you are building a relationship. A good relationship is based on honesty.

6. Do not use foul language. Do not tell or listen to offensive jokes. You may find it necessary to change the subject or leave if inappropriate conversation arises.

7. Do not brag. Bragging can cause jealousy.

8. Do not tattle or tease. Others will appreciate you more if you are sensitive to how they are feeling.

9. Do not contradict or correct others in public. This discourtesy is disrespectful to adults and can be offensive to friends.

10. Do not complain about chores, food, or not getting your way.

11. Do not display emotional outbursts of anger.

"Wherefore, my beloved brethren, let every man be swift to hear, slow to speak, slow to wrath: for the wrath of man worketh not the righteousness of God."
James 1:19-20 KJV

~ Conversation ~

Friendship

(One way)

Oops and her friend Alexandria see one another after school and stop to talk.

Oops: Hey, Alexandria.

Alexandria: (Looking sad) Oh, hi.

Oops: What's up?

Alexandria: Nothing, I guess.

Oops: Yes, there is. I can tell.

Alexandria: Well, you know I tried out for the play that Mrs. Stagemaster is doing.

Oops: Oh, I remember . . . wasn't it *The Spoons That Do Lunch*? No wait . . . don't tell me . . . I know. It's *The Forks That Came To Dinner*. That's right. O.K., so what happened with that?

Alexandria: I didn't get a part.

Oops: You know, you're really good, Alexandria. What does Mrs. Stagemaster know about your talents anyway?

Alexandria: I don't know, but I really wanted to be in the play.

Oops: You shouldn't be upset; you'd have to go to rehearsals and learn all those lines. We can find some fun things to do.

Alexandria: (Walking away) Yeah, I guess so. See you later, Oops.

Oops: I'll call you.

Alexandria: (To herself) You know, I don't feel much better.

~ Conversation ~

Friendship

(Let's try again)

Oops: Hey, Alexandria.

Alexandria: (Looking sad) Oh, hi.

Oops: Are you all right?

Alexandria: Not really. I talked to Mrs. Stagemaster.

Oops: What did she say to make you so upset?

Alexandria: I didn't get a part in *The Forks That Came To Dinner.*

Oops: Oh, I know you must be disappointed.

Alexandria: I really wanted to be in the play.

Oops: I'm sorry, Alexandria.

Alexandria: Thanks, Oops, but I'll be O.K. It does make me feel better that Mrs. Stagemaster asked me to try out for her next play.

Oops: That's sounds encouraging. I'll help you with your lines for the next audition. I have to meet my mom in a few minutes. I'll ask her if you can spend the night tonight.

Alexandria: That would be fun. See you later, Oops.

Oops: I'll call you.

Alexandria: (To herself) You know, I'm still disappointed, but Oops seems to understand and care how I feel. I hope I'll see her later tonight. Maybe Oops is learning something in that manners class after all.

Conversation Facts

I remember the ___ ___ ___ ___ ___ about conversation.

F un
A ttention
C ompliments
T hank you
S peak

News Article

Conversation Acrostic

Fill in the acrostic with the correct answer to the clue below.

1. Rise and say "_____" as someone leaves your house.

2. It is not polite to _____ secrets in front of others.

3. Interrupt conversation only when _____.

4. _____ polite questions to help get to know someone.

5. Everyone is worthy of _____.

6. If a friend approaches you when you are talking, he _____ be included in the conversation.

7. When bumping into someone, say, "_____ _____."

8. Look for opportunities to give sincere _____.

9. When sneezing, cover your mouth and _____ your head.

10. Do not contradict or _____ your parents in public.

CONVERSATION ENHANCER: ___ __ __ __ __ __ __   __ __ __ __

Telephone Etiquette

Jeremiah 33:3

Call unto me, and I will answer thee, and shew
thee great and mighty things, which thou knowest
not.

King James Version

Call to me and I will answer you and tell you great
and unsearchable things you do not know.

New International Version

38

Telephone Etiquette

A telephone call is an entrance into the home. Show consideration to those calling your home as you would to a guest. Respect those in the homes you call.

ANSWERING THE TELEPHONE

1. Say, **"Hello"** (not yeah or yo).

2. If the call is not for you, say, **"One moment, please"** or **"Just a minute, please."** Expressions such as **"Hang on"** or **"Hold on"** sound like commands.

3. Immediately notify the recipient of the call. Avoid shouting when you let someone know she has a call. Set the telephone down **g_____** and then look for the person receiving the call.

4. Do not demand to know who is calling or what she wants. Examples - Who is this? Whatdayawant? Say: **"May I tell my mother who's calling?"** Ask this question to inform the person called, not to satisfy your own curiosity.

5. If the caller is a family member or friend, say a few cordial words before handing over the telephone. **"How are you feeling today, Mamaw?"**

6. Hang up as soon as you hear the recipient speak to the caller from another telephone.

7. Sometimes more than one person will answer the telephone at the same time. Hearing several voices at once is confusing to the caller. Determine who should hang up and who should take the call. It may be better to let the adult or older child in the house take the call. You may want to ask your parents what you should do.

8. If the person called is not available:

    ◆ DO NOT tell the caller that there is no one else at home! (a good safety rule)
    ◆ Say - **"He cannot come to the telephone right now. May I take a message or ask him to return your call?"**
    ◆ Write down the message right away. Repeat the message to the caller to assure its accuracy. Deliver the message as soon as possible.

9.   Ask your parents about the safety rules of your home.

   ◆What information to give those who call your home
   ◆When and how to use 911
   ◆When and how to use the internet

MAKING A TELEPHONE CALL

1.   Think about your call before you dial the number. Have a good idea of what you want to say before you call someone. The person you are calling will not appreciate having to wait while you decide.

2.   Do not call before 9:00 a.m. or after 9:00 or 9:30 p.m.

3.   Avoid calling others as they are beginning their day. They may be trying to leave for work or getting ready for school.

4.   Allow six rings before hanging up.

5.   Identify yourself. **"This is _____. May I please speak to _____?"**

6.   If someone you know answers, say a word of greeting especially to parents. **"Hello, Mrs. Hamilton. This is Oops. May I speak to Alexandria?"**

7.   Ask the person you are calling if she is busy. Be sensitive to her situation if you have called at an inconvenient time. She may have company, be involved in a project, or need to leave shortly. **"I'm sorry for the interruption; please call me later about our Manners Class."**

8.   Be prepared to speak to a recording. If your call is received by an answering machine leave your name, the time of your call, brief information regarding your reason for calling, your telephone number, a thank you and a goodbye.

9.   Apologize for wrong numbers:

   ◆**"Please excuse the interruption."**
   ◆**"I'm sorry I have the wrong number."**
   ◆**"I was trying to reach 555-6677."**

10.   Avoid picking up the telephone to see if there is a conversation on the line. Check the other telephones in the house before attempting to make your call.

11. Return calls promptly.

12. Ending the telephone call is generally the responsibility of the **c**_____.

CONVERSATION ON THE TELEPHONE

1. Speak clearly. The person on the other end cannot see your facial expressions. Your voice alone must convey your words and feelings.

2. Avoid eating, chewing gum, or making noises with paper, pencils, or other items.

3. Be attentive. Avoid talking to others in the room while you are on the telephone. Excuse yourself if you must speak to someone else.
"Excuse me, my mom needs to ask me something."

4. Do not encourage conversation when you have company.
"Please excuse me, I have company. May I call you later?"

5. Be aware of your time spent on the telephone. It is important to be considerate of others who need to use the telephone.

6. Always end with **"Goodbye."**

SOMEONE ELSE IS USING THE TELEPHONE

1. Be considerate of others by allowing them privacy.

2. Keep your interruptions to a minimum.

3. Avoid making unnecessary noises near someone who is on the telephone.

CALL WAITING

1. If your conversation is interrupted by call waiting, either disregard the second call or say, **"I have another call; could you hold please?"**

2. Do not keep anyone holding for long. After taking the second call say, **"I'm sorry; could I call you back? I'm on the other line."**

3. When expecting a call, say, **"I may need to take another call in a few minutes."**

43

PUBLIC TELEPHONES

1.   Remember that a public telephone is provided as a convenience for necessary calls. Be brief.

2.   Be aware of someone else's need for privacy while he is using the telephone. Do not hover over him while you are waiting to use the telephone.

3.   It is often difficult to hear while using public telephones. Avoid making unnecessary noise.

OBSCENE CALLS

1.   It is not impolite to hang up immediately when you realize the call is obscene.

2.   Tell your parents about the call.

3.   If the calls continue, ask your parents what you should do.

The Polite SCRAMBLE

Unscramble these words that refer to Telephone Etiquette. Use the circled letters to form two new words.

1. rsepcet ◯ __ __ __ __ __ __

2. wrtei __ __ __ ◯ __

3. angh pu __ __ ◯ __ __ ◯ __

4. pptmor __ ◯ __ __ __ __

5. ypvacri __ __ __ __ ◯ __ __

6. holel __ ◯ __ ◯ __

7. creally __ __ __ __ __ ◯ __

8. lacl ◯ __ __ __

When you use good telephone etiquette, you receive a:

__ __ __ __ __ __ __   __ __ __ __.

Guest Relations

Oops, It's Your Birthday

Philippians 1:27a

Only let your conversation be as it becometh the gospel of Christ.

King James Version

Whatever happens, conduct yourselves in a manner worthy of the gospel of Christ.

New International Version

48

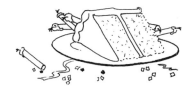

Guest Relations

You Are the Host

Your entertaining may be a casual gathering of friends for pizza, a birthday party, or a formal dinner for a large group. A good host can make the difference in the comfort and enjoyment of the guests on any occasion.

THE INVITATION

1. Carefully consider your guest list. Will those whom you plan to include enjoy their time together?

2. Make every effort to send invitations or call those on your guest list on the same day.

3. Send invitations or call ten days to three weeks ahead; four to six weeks ahead for more formal occasions such as weddings. Giving plenty of advance notice is helpful to others so they can make plans to attend.

4. Be specific when giving information. Include the exact time, place, date, day of the week, names of those hosting the event, the occasion, directions or a map, and indicate if it is a surprise.

5. Instead of asking what someone is doing on a certain date, just extend the invitation.

6. When people inform you that they are unable to attend, let them know you are sorry that they cannot come and that they will be missed.

7. If someone wants to bring a friend and you choose to include her, extend a personal invitation to the friend.

BEFORE THE GUESTS ARRIVE

1. Make preparations as much in advance as possible, such as, cleaning the house, rearranging the furniture, decorating the party area, setting the table, preparing the food, making name tags, and getting your clothes ready. Preparing ahead will allow you time to focus more attention on your guests.

49

2. It is a good idea to be ready for your guests at least 30 minutes ahead of time.
    a. **What time is your party scheduled to begin?**_____
    b. **How long does it take you to get dressed?** _____
    c. **Do you have last minute preparations? How long will these preparations take?** _____
    d. **Add:** 30 minutes   - _____
              getting dressed   - _____
              preparations   - _____
                      Total - _____
    e. **Subtract the total of "d" from the time of your party.**
        _____ **is the time to begin getting ready for your guests.**

3. If you have a family pet, consider taking him to another room or outside when guests visit. How can you tell if it is necessary to move your pet? Notice how your guest responds when you say, "Oh, I'll just let Bow Wow the Dog play outside."
    What does your guest say?
    a. ____ **Nothing.**
    b. ____ **"Bye, bye, Bow Wow."**
    c. ____ **"Oh no please . . . I love Bow Wow the Dog. Let him stay so we may grow closer."**
    d. ____ **"Please don't put Bow Wow out on my account."**
    Unless you check c or d, Bow Wow should bow out.

THE GUESTS ARRIVE

1. Welcome and introduce all guests as they arrive. Provide a convenient place such as a coat closet or bedroom for coats, sweaters, purses and other belongings. Offer refreshments.

2. Divide your time equally among your guests and insure that conversation flows smoothly during your party. Avoid spending most of your time with one person.

3. Guests appreciate your consideration for their comfort by keeping your house neither too hot nor too cold.

4. Keep an eye on the food and drink supply.

5. Playing games or planning special activities can add enjoyment to your party. Be considerate, however, of those who do not wish to participate.

6. Give attention to the atmosphere of your party, and be ready to change your plans if a number of the guests are not enjoying the game or activity. If everyone is having a good time, you may want to delay other planned activities.

7.   Give preference to your guests whether you are serving food, playing a game, or participating in some activity. The hospitality you offer your guests is more important than the table decorations, the appearance of your house, or the food you serve.

8.   When receiving a gift, open the card first and read it. After opening the gift, thank the person and mention something positive about the gift to show your appreciation.

9.   If you have unexpected guests, try to make them feel as welcome as possible under the circumstances.

10.   If your parents are entertaining and you are not included in the party, be courteous and friendly but avoid trying to be the center of attention. Before guests arrive, ask your parents where you should be during the party.

THE GUESTS LEAVE

1.   As each guest leaves, go to the door with him. Tell him goodbye and let him know you are glad he came.

2.   If you received gifts, thank the giver again and name the gift if possible.

3.   Walk your guest to his car to enjoy a few last moments together, unless you would be neglecting other guests by doing so.

THE OVERNIGHT VISITOR

1.   If you entertain guests overnight, consider needs they may have and provide for them in advance. Furnish clothes hangers, and allow space for hanging clothes. Supply fresh towels and linens and an alarm clock. Clean the bathroom and bedroom.

2.   In a small basket, arrange sample size personal items, such as a new toothbrush and toothpaste, for your guests to use.

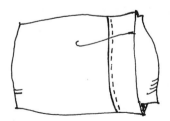

51

You Are the Guest

You may be invited to a casual get-together at someone's home or for an overnight visit. In either case, being a pleasant guest is just as important as being a delightful host.

THE INVITATION

1. After receiving an invitation, respond within two or three days. Let the person know you appreciate the invitation and are looking forward to the event.

2. You will sometimes find R.S.V.P. written on the invitation. R.S.V.P. is an abbreviation for French words that mean "Please reply."

3. If the R.S.V.P. includes "Regrets only," respond if you are unable to attend.

4. Whenever you decline an invitation, thank the person for inviting you. Briefly explain why you are unable to attend.

5. When writing a response to a formal invitation, use paper of a stationary quality and a black pen.

6. If you or a member of your party must cancel, inform the hostess as soon as you know.

7. Never cancel because you later receive a "better" offer.

8. Do not go if you are sick.

9. Do not drop in uninvited.

BEFORE YOU ARRIVE

1. Never take a pet unless the host has extended the invitation.

2. Always be on time. If you are running more than a few minutes late, call the hostess to let her know. On the other hand, a hostess usually likes those last few minutes to be sure that everything is in order, and an early guest can make last minute preparations difficult.

3. Knock on the door and wait for an answer.

    ◆ If you are attending a birthday celebration, wish the guest of honor a happy birthday if she answers the door.

◆If you do not know the person answering the door, introduce yourself.

DURING THE VISIT

1. Ask the hostess, "How may I help?"

2. Respect the home you are visiting.

    ◆Wipe your shoes before entering.
    ◆Keep your feet off the furniture.
    ◆Do not ask for food or drink. If you are thirsty, ask for water.
    ◆Put away what you use.
    ◆If your hands are dirty, wash them before using a towel.
    ◆Do not slam doors or run up and down the stairs.
    ◆Do not answer the door or the telephone unless you have been asked to do so.

3. If hors d' oeuvres are served:

    ◆Napkins or coasters should be accessible when beverages are served. If they are not, be careful where you set your drink. Moisture from the glass may damage the furniture.
    ◆Place foods on a plate instead of eating directly from the table.
    ◆Place stems, pits, seeds, and toothpicks in your napkin unless something else is provided.
    ◆Do not spoil your appetite for a meal.

4. Respect the privacy of your host. Do not enter a room if the door is closed. Do not look through drawers or closets. Do not use his personal items.

5. Participate in all the activities that are presented for entertainment. Do your best to have a good time even if you do not prefer the game or activity. Do not turn on the television unless you are asked to do so.

END OF THE VISIT

1. Be aware of the time so you will not stay too long, even if others are staying.

2. Offer to help clean up dishes or other items that may need to be put away. Collect your belongings.

3. Thank the hostess for a good time.

4. The next day, call the hostess or send a note to say how much you enjoyed the the party.

53

AN OVERNIGHT VISIT

1. Greet the family, but mainly visit with your host.

2. Avoid comparing how things are done at your house. Notice how the host and the rest of the family operate and try to fit in.

   * Honor the curfew.
   * Keep your voice down.
   * Ignore family disagreements.

3. Keep your personal items neat and tidy. Clean up after yourself and put away things that you use.

   * Bring a plastic bag for swim clothes.
   * Make your bed.
   * Hang up your towel after using it.
   * Offer to help.

4. If you were invited for a specified period of time, do not stay longer.

5. Thank the host for his hospitality.

6. Send a thank you note as soon as you return home.

7. For weekend visits, it is thoughtful to take a family gift. Examples: games, plants, music, candy, books, note pads, coasters, subscription to a magazine of interest, gift certificate for a restaurant.

"Above all, love each other deeply, because love covers over a multitude of sins. Offer hospitality to one another without grumbling." I Peter 4:8-9 NIV

Punch Recipe

Build An Invitation

Invitations

Formal

Mr. and Mrs. Mark Oopsman
request the pleasure of your company
at dinner
on Saturday, the thirtieth of March
at seven o'clock
711 Hosting Drive

R.S.V.P.

Response card (Send with a self-addressed stamped envelope.)

The favor of a reply is
requested before the
fifteenth of March
M _____
will _____ *attend*

Informal:

FOR _____

DATE _____

TIME _____

PLACE _____

GIVEN BY _____

R.S.V.P. 555-6677

56

Formal Reply to Invitation

Mr. and Mrs. Moses Valentine
regret they are unable to accept
the kind invitation of
Mr. and Mrs. Oopsman
to dinner
on Saturday, the thirtieth of March

Mr. Moses Valentine
accepts with pleasure
the kind invitation of
Mr. and Mrs. Mark Oopsman
to dinner
on Saturday, the thirtieth of March
at seven o'clock
but regrets that
Mrs. Valentine
will be unable to attend
due to a previous appointment

Hosting - Multiple Choice

Write the letter(s) with the correct answer(s) to each number.

_____ **1.** Good guest relations should be used
    a. only in your Manners Class.
    b. only at formal dinners.
    c. whether you are the host or the guest.

_____ **2.** Call or send invitations
    a. 10 months to three years ahead.
    b. 10 weeks to three months ahead.
    c. 10 days to three weeks ahead.

_____ **3.** What does R.S.V.P. mean?
    a. Respond please, by letting the hostess know as soon as possible if she should expect you.
    b. Tell everyone else if you will be attending and let it get around to the hostess.
    c. Respond if and when you get around to it.

_____ **4.** When playing party games,
    a. hide in your room unless everyone participates.
    b. call the parents of those who will not participate.
    c. be considerate of those who do not wish to participate.

_____ **5.** What is the MOST important thing you can offer your guests?
    a. Delicious food
    b. Great prizes
    c. Hospitality

~ Guest Relations ~

_____ **6.** As guests leave,
    a. go to the door with each one.
    b. tell each one goodbye.
    c. ask each one how much was spent on your gift.

_____ **7.** If your parents are entertaining guests,
    a. show what you learned in Karate class.
    b. ask your parents where you should be during the party.
    c. go to your bedroom and play your music so loudly that no one will forget about you.

_____ **8.** During the visit,
    a. respect the home in which you are visiting.
    b. feel free to use the host's toothbrush, perfume, or any other items you want.
    c. clean up after yourself.

_____ **9.** When birthday cake is being cut,
    a. run to the cake and get the first piece.
    b. say, "I'm sorry to be a pig, but may I have another piece."
    c. wait until you are served or asked to serve yourself.

_____**10.** When visiting overnight,
    a. tell the family what you do at home so that they may adjust and be better hosts.
    b. provide the host with a grocery list of your favorite junk foods.
    c. thank the host for having you.

Manners
Away from Home

I Peter 2:17

Honour all men. Love the brotherhood. Fear God. Honour the king.   King James Version

Show proper respect to everyone: Love the brotherhood of believers, fear God, honor the king.   New International Version

Manners Away from Home

RIDING IN THE CAR

When others are riding in your car, put forth every effort to make them feel welcome. When you are riding in someone else's car, there are important things to remember about showing courtesy and appreciation.

1. It is not impolite to refuse rides from strangers.

2. Fasten your seat belt.

3. Greet others in the car.

4. Abide by the rules of the driver.

   ◆ Avoid demanding a certain seat.
   ◆ Keep your voice down.
   ◆ Do not eat or drink without permission.

5. Help to make the ride pleasant for everyone. Avoid continuous questions such as "Are we there yet?"

6. Gather your belongings before leaving the car.

7. Thank the driver for the ride. If you travel a long distance, write a t_____ you note.

8. Say goodbye to everyone.

ATTENDING CHURCH

Whether you are a member or visitor, show reverence and respect as you worship God with others.

1. Have your drink of water and take care of other personal needs before entering a worship service. Leaving during worship disturbs others.

2. It is "Ladies first" into the row to be seated.

3. Make room for others.

4. Be careful with the song books and other property.
   Do not use the seat in front of you as a foot rest.

63

5. Do not talk during worship or during a presentation in any setting.

6. It is inappropriate to pass notes to your friends during the worship service.

7. Take an active role as a volunteer in your church. Examples: Help in the nursery and with summer programs. Help your teacher in class and clean up areas where you see litter or things out of place.

There are always opportunities in God's work; you are never too old or too young to serve.

PARTICIPATING IN SPORTS

The purpose of sports is to enjoy the game. Give your best effort and help everyone else have fun.

1. Be on time.

2. Follow the rules of the game.

3. Do not cheat.

4. Resolve disagreements peacefully.

5. Do not try to tell others how to play.

6. Encourage others. When someone executes a good play, say, "Good shot." When someone misses or sends the ball into a neighboring field or court, do not make a "big deal" out of it. Say, "Next time" or "Good try."

7. During the transfer of the ball for the next play, either hand, roll, or carefully toss the ball to someone. Never throw it at someone and then laugh when it hits him in the face.

8. If someone is hurt during play, ask if he is all right and help with first aid when necessary.

9. Good sportsmanship is not determined by whether you win or lose the game. Being a "good sport," however, may determine whether or not you are asked to play again.

♦ It is not impolite to be excited about winning. Winners, however, should never boast about their victory. Compliment the other team or player. You are insulting yourself when you suggest the other person is not a good player.
♦ If you are on the losing team, always congratulate the winners.

64

♦Do not express your disappointment by throwing the ball, bat, or cap. Do not blame the loss on your teammates or "bad luck."

10. Whether you are a player or spectator, do not insult the umpire, players, or spectators.

11. Be considerate of others who may be waiting for the playing area by finishing your game in a timely manner. Do not show impatience while waiting for others to finish their game. Wait to be invited before joining a game in progress.

BEING COURTEOUS AWAY FROM HOME

1. Respect public property.

    ♦Follow the rules. Examples: Keep off the grass. Do not touch the exhibits. Stay behind the line and wait to be called. Once you leave, do not attempt to re-enter. Do not bring food or drink into the store. Please speak softly.
    ♦Put litter in its place.
    ♦Please do not write on or destroy public property.

2. Respect those with whom you share this world.

    ♦Offer your seat and hold the door for anyone in need. Examples: Politely move over if two friends want to sit together. Hold the door for an older person, someone with special needs, a pregnant lady, a small child, or someone carrying a baby.
    ♦If someone near you drops something, pick it up and hand it back.
    ♦If someone behind you in line has only a few items, let the person go in front of you. Also, do not cut in line.
    ♦Keep your feet out of the aisle.
    ♦If you are walking with several people, make room for others who may want to pass.
    ♦Enjoy your day at the park or beach. Take just the space you need. Clean up for the next person to enjoy.

3. Be considerate of others when you are entering or exiting an elevator.

    ♦Hold the "open" button if you see someone trying to enter the elevator.
    ♦Press the elevator button and step aside to allow others room to step out of the elevator before you enter. Who gets off first? It is "Ladies first." If the elevator is crowded, the closest person to the door steps out first.
    ♦It is "Ladies first" through the revolving door.

4.   Boys remove their hats when they are indoors.

  ◆There are a few exceptions.
  ◆A lady may keep her hat on unless it blocks the vision of someone sitting behind her.

ATTENDING SCHOOL

Take pride in your school, which is here for you and those who come after you. Most of your day is spent at school. As you attend, how can you contribute to making this time a pleasant learning experience for yourself and others?

1.   Practice good study habits.

  ◆Organize your work.
  ◆Complete your homework without being reminded.
  ◆Be willing to help classmates without boasting about your accomplishments.
  ◆Be prepared for class with your books, paper, pencil, and completed homework.

2.   Listen carefully in class.

  ◆Listening will help you prepare for tests. When you listen, you encourage others to listen. Your teachers are encouraged when they see your interest in learning.
  ◆Participate in class.
  ◆Do not interrupt others. Raise your hand and wait until the teacher calls on you.

3.   Show courtesy, consideration, and respect to teachers, staff, classmates, and guests.

  ◆Introduce yourself to new students and include them in conversation.
  ◆Follow school polices as well as the rules of your classroom. When asked to control your behavior, do so right away.
  ◆Limit your complaints and talk with your teacher in private about disagreements.

4.   Use good table manners during lunch. Friends eating with you will appreciate your consideration. Throw away your trash before leaving the lunchroom.

5.   Spend only the time needed in the restroom. Clean up after yourself.

6.   Follow the safety rules of the playground and take turns.

7.   The library is a quiet place. Be considerate of others who are reading and studying. Take care of the books and return them when they are due.

"When wisdom entereth into thine heart, and knowledge is pleasing unto thy soul; discretion shall preserve thee, understanding shall keep thee."
Proverbs 2:10-11 KJV

The Away from Home Challenge

Riding in a Car	Attending Church	Playing Sports	Being Courteous
1. Is it a good idea to always grab your favorite seat?	1. If you use the seat in front of you as a foot rest, will the minister think you are enjoying the sermon?	1. Should you insist on telling others how to play, showing them what they are doing wrong?	1. Is holding the door for someone just an old tradition?
2. Should you surprise the driver by bringing plenty of food?	2. If you offer to help a teacher in class or to volunteer in the nursery, will people think you are in the way?	2. Is skill in throwing the ball the only sign of being a "good sport?"	2. Is littering the ground a good way to create jobs for people?
3. Is it a good idea to refuse rides from strangers?	3. During a presentation, speech, or worship service should you and your friends practice the conversation lesson?	3. Will giving your best effort add to the enjoyment of the game for others?	3. If you suddenly feel inspired to write a poem or paint a beautiful picture on a public building, does this destroy property?

67

Table Manners

Galatians 5:13b

By love serve one another. King James Version

Serve one another in love. New International Version

I Corinthians 13:5

(charity) doth not behave itself unseemly, seeketh not her own, is not easily provoked, thinketh no evil. King James Version

(Love) is not rude, it is not self-seeking, it is not easily angered, it keeps no record of wrongs. New International Version

Table Manners

Use table manners to aid in the enjoyment and digestion of meals for yourself and those eating with you. A child whose good table manners are showing will be more comfortable and welcomed when eating with adults, friends, and family.

WHEN MINNIE FRENZ CALLS OR VISITS DURING DINNER?

1. Telephone calls during dinner may be returned later. Let the caller know you are having dinner and will call back after the meal.

2. Visitors may be invited to eat or to wait.

3. As a visitor, it is best not to join the meal unless you know the family well. It is appropriate to accept an offer of dessert.

WHAT TO SAY

1. Enjoy pleasant conversation with those sitting close to you when you are at a large dinner party.

2. Make an effort to speak to everyone in a small group setting.

3. Avoid arguing, complaining about the meal, complaining in general, or being too descriptive about the food. Anything that in any way keeps someone from enjoying the meal is **o**_____ **o**_____ **p**_____ at the table.

4. Be aware of facial expressions and reactions of others. Please do not continue when others show they are not pleased with the conversation.

5. Be complimentary about the meal, the table setting, etc. The hostess should not ask the guests their opinion of the food.

HOW TO SIT

1. Let the back of your knees touch the chair.

2. Sit down, keeping your body straight.

3.   Slide back carefully in your chair.

4.   Keep your legs straight down and still.

5.   Be relaxed, but do not lean the chair back.

6.   Sit a few inches from the table and lean slightly forward. Do not lean into your plate as you eat.

7.   Do not rest your elbows on the table as if you are trying to balance your head. Elbows are allowed at the table's edge only between courses and when the meal is finished mainly to aid in listening to conversation.

8.   Place your hands in your lap when you are not eating, especially when you are at a formal dinner.

WHERE TO SIT

1.   The hostess goes to the table first and lets the guests know where to sit unless there are place cards. At a large gathering, the hostess may place a seating chart where it can be seen easily by guests.

2.   Sit at your usual place for family meals.

3.   Your parent will show a guest where to sit. There may be a change in family seating when guests are present.

WHEN TO SIT

1.   Go to the table with a neat, clean appearance.

2.   Be seated when the hostess sits or asks you to sit. (Before this time, wait behind the chair.)

3.   Gentlemen wait for ladies to sit and may pull out the chair for ladies near them, pushing the chairs in as the ladies sit. Gentlemen may also help ladies with their chairs at the end of the meal.

WHEN TO START EATING

1.   Wait for the hostess to ask for the blessing. If a minister is present, he should be asked to say the blessing or grace. If no blessing is offered, discreetly offer thanks on your own.

2. Place the napkin in your lap and begin eating when the hostess starts unless she asks you to start without her.

3. If the hostess is distracted, wait until those at your table are seated and begin eating before you start eating. In a small group, wait until everyone is served.

4. A child should wait for the adults beside him before he begins.

5. If an expected guest is late, wait about 15 minutes and then proceed with the meal. If he comes in later, he sits in on the course being served when he arrives. If he has missed the entire meal, the hostess may provide him with a plate of food.

THE PASSING GAME

1. At a formal dinner, guests are served. Serving dishes are not placed on the table. Serving dishes are on the table, however, and passed from person to person for family style dining.

2. Whether formal or family style, the main course is passed first.

3. Dishes are usually passed counterclockwise (to the right) or at least passed in the same direction.

4. A gentleman serves himself and may hold the dish for the lady next to him. Anyone may hold the platter for the next person if it is hard to hold.

5. Mothers may fill the plates of her family, but guests should be allowed to serve themselves.

TAKING FOOD FROM THE SERVING DISH

1. When taking a portion of food from a serving dish, use the serving silverware on the dish or tray and replace it face down. Place the handles where the next person may use the silverware easily and where it will not fall while it is passed.

2. If two utensils are provided, place the spoon under the food and the fork on the top (tines down) to move it to your plate.

3. Take the portion closest to you and keep it if you touch it.

4. Take a medium amount. You will leave enough for others and also will be taking enough to compliment the hostess.

5.   Take a little of everything. Be adventurous and willing to try different foods. It is acceptable to politely refuse foods that you are unable to eat. If the hostess offers food, place it on your plate.

6.   Take all the portion of food if it is served as a whole piece. You may also take some of the seasoning or sauce around it.

7.   Pour gravies onto the meat and potatoes. Place more solid condiments such as preserves next to foods to which they are added.

SALT AND PEPPER

1.   Pass the salt and pepper as a set.

2.   At a formal dinner, a set is usually provided for every other place. At least one salt and pepper set should be provided for every eight diners. Use salt and pepper sparingly.

3.   Avoid asking for seasoning that is not on the table. It is appropriate to butter foods such as bread, corn on the cob, and baked potatoes. Taste your food before adding seasoning.

SECOND HELPINGS

1.   Do not ask for seconds when the food is not on the table. You may accept seconds if they are offered to you.

2.   When food is on the table, wait for a break in conversation and then politely ask the closest person, "Would you pass the rolls, please?" Then thank him. Do not say, "Pass some rolls" or "Rolls." Avoid just pointing to rolls or other food items.

3.   Serve yourself if a dish of food is near you and will not require your reaching in front of someone. Offer the food to the diners on both sides of you before serving yourself.

4.   You may pass your plate to be filled. Leave the silverware carefully balanced toward the middle of the plate.

5.   As a dish is passed to someone requesting it, you may ask to take some of the food as it is passed, unless there is not enough.

6.   At a formal dinner where there are several courses, you will probably have enough food by the meal's end. If the guest of honor asks for another helping, the other guests will probably be offered one also.

~ Table Manners ~

THE BUFFET

The buffet gives guests the opportunity to choose favorite foods and visit around the room.

1. Place the buffet table in the middle of the room for a large crowd so two lines may be served at once, or place the table against the wall. Arrange the setting so the guests may choose everything they want and need and may easily pass to the seating.

2. Elderly guests may go through the line first or younger guests may go through the line for them and bring them filled plates. A child lets adults go ahead of him, and a gentleman lets a lady go ahead.

3. It is better to return to the buffet for more food than to overfill your plate.

4. The hostess stands by the buffet table and supplies the food as needed.

    ◆The hostess may pour the drinks after the guests are seated and during the meal.
    ◆It is nice to serve the dessert so the guests will not have to return to the buffet table after the main course.

5. In a restaurant, you may order the buffet while others with whom you are dining order from the menu. Time your trip to the buffet line so that you will have your meal at the same time the others are served.

Watch the Hostess

Hostess

Sit

Blessing

Napkin

Eating

Talk

Leave

75

Copyright © 1997, 1999 The Oops Group, Inc. Not to be reproduced.

SOME FINGER FOODS

Apples - Quarter the apple, remove the core and cut the apple into slices.

Artichokes - Dip each leaf into the sauce; pull the leaf between your teeth; cut away the choke with a knife; cut the heart into small pieces; eat the heart with a fork and knife, dipping the heart into the sauce.

Asparagus - If the asparagus is firm and covered with little or no sauce, you may eat the asparagus with your fingers. (There may be a sauce for dipping.)

Crisp bacon

Bananas - Break a banana into bite size pieces.

Corn on the cob - Butter the corn with a knife, a few rows at a time to limit the amount of dripping.

 Fried Chicken - You may eat fried chicken with your fingers when dining outdoors or when dining in a family style setting. (Follow the example of the hostess.)

Grapes - Break off one small branch at a time and eat the grapes from it.

Sandwiches - A large sandwich cut in half is easier to eat.

Shrimp - When shrimp is served in the shell, peel away the shell and press the tail to push the meat forward and out.

Strawberries - Hold a strawberry by the hull to eat it.

Tangerines - Peel and section the tangerine.

76

Oops at the Table!

YOUR FOOD IS TOO HOT

1. Consider that your food may be too hot before eating it.

2. Drink something cold if you have taken a bite of hot food.

A CREATURE OR OBJECT WANTS TO SHARE YOUR MEAL

1. If you notice an unwelcome object on your plate, quietly ask the hostess for a replacement.

2. If the hostess realizes the problem and offers you another dish, accept it.

3. In a restaurant, quietly ask the waiter for a replacement. The other guests should not ask why.

YOU DO NOT LIKE OR CANNOT EAT A CERTAIN FOOD

1. Try a few bites.

2. Eat around the food.

YOU NEED TO REMOVE SOMETHING FROM YOUR MOUTH

1. Remove most food items with the tip of your silverware or fingers (however it went in).

2. Remove small bones or shells with your fingers.

3. Remove food that has been chewed with your spoon or fork.

4. Pits may go into your loosely held fist or your spoon.

5. After removing the food item, place it on the side of the dinner plate or bread and butter plate.

6. If it is unsightly, cover it with food on the side of your plate.

SOMETHING IS STUCK IN YOUR TEETH

1.   Ignore it.

2.   Try to work it out with your tongue.

3.   Drink water.

4.   Excuse yourself from the table and privately remove the item by using a toothpick, dental floss, or by swishing water around in your mouth.

YOU ARE ASKED A QUESTION WHEN YOU HAVE A FULL MOUTH

1.   Do not talk with food in your mouth.

2.   Avoid putting too much food in your mouth at once. Smaller bites can be swallowed more quickly, allowing you to answer.

3.   Continue chewing normally.

4.   Smile and point to your mouth.

5.   Hope that someone says something to redirect the conversation.

YOU MUST TAKE CARE OF SOMETHING PERSONAL

1.   Try to wait until the end of the meal.

2.   If you cannot wait, excuse yourself.

3.   There is no need to give the reason.

YOU BREAK SOMETHING

1.   Apologize.

2.   Buy a replacement or pay for the damage. Repair irreplaceable items.

3.   Send a gift and note of regret.

~ Table Manners ~

YOU DROP YOUR NAPKIN ON THE FLOOR

1. In an informal setting, quietly pick up your napkin up.

2. In a formal setting, whether in a restaurant or home, the server may pick it up for you. Quietly pick up the napkin yourself if the server does not.

YOU DROP FOOD ON THE FLOOR

1. Leave it until after the meal unless it will damage the flooring.

2. Let the hostess or waiter know if it could cause someone to fall.

3. In most cases, the hostess or waiter will clean the area when the guests leave.

YOU DROP SILVERWARE ON THE FLOOR

1. In someone's home, pick it up if you can easily reach it. Set it aside and ask for another if the silverware is needed for the meal.

2. In a restaurant, ask for more silverware.

YOU SPILL FOOD OR DRINK ON THE TABLE

1. Remove it with a clean knife or spoon, or dry it with your napkin.

2. Let the hostess know about it if damage will be done.

3. If the hostess is aware of the spill, she will probably clean it.

YOU SPILL FOOD OR DRINK ON SOMEONE

1. Act quickly.

2. Clean it as well as you can.

3. Have his clothes professionally cleaned if necessary.

4. Apologize and continue the meal.

YOU SPILL FOOD OR DRINK ON YOURSELF

1. Remove the spill with a clean knife or spoon.

2. Use the tip of your napkin to wipe the spill.

   Whatever the "oops," do not continue discussing how badly you feel about it.

Formal Seating Diagram

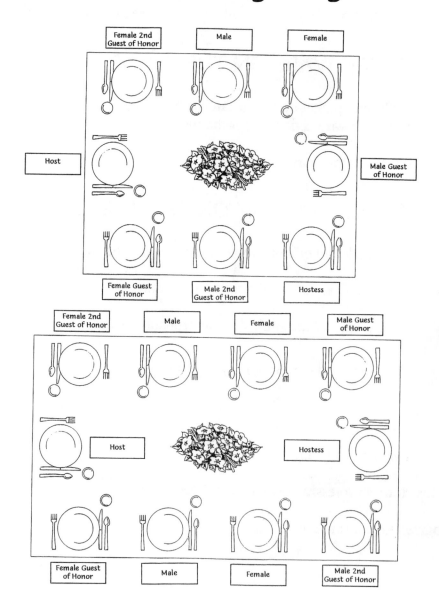

Manners Word Search

Help good table manners to show. Draw a loop around the hidden words that are needed to fill in the blanks of the sentences below. The words are in straight lines: three vertical words, three horizonal words, three diagonal words (from the direction of the upper left hand corner).

```
W  A  I  T  L  H  H  B  M  H  G  A  H  T
R  E  M  O  T  B  O  M  T  B  A  B  X  H
Z  Z  Z  B  L  E  S  S  I  N  G  C  X  A
Z  P  R  W  B  B  T  Z  N  S  Z  D  P  N
Z  A  A  L  O  P  E  P  S  P  T  E  L  K
L  B  E  S  A  X  S  Y  A  I  O  Y  G  Z
A  C  A  E  S  I  S  X  B  O  T  G  L  A
P  D  B  T  F  M  Z  T  C  U  X  Z  J  E
P  E  U  P  X  B  K  R  D  L  O  Z  P  E
B  U  F  F  E  T  Z  T  E  P  Z  G  X  U
```

Please __ __ __ __ up straight in your chair and __ __ __ __ __ __ until the

__ __ __ __ __ __ __ __ __ asks for the __ __ __ __ __ __ __ __ __ to be said before placing the

napkin in your __ __ __ __. Whether the meal is formal, a __ __ __ __ __ __ __ with a serving

line, or served family __ __ __ __ __ __ __, where you __ __ __ __ __ __ the food, remember to

__ __ __ __ __ __ your hostess.

At Your Service

Keep these rules in mind whenever you are serving guests and want to make their meal enjoyable.

1. Serve the female guest of honor first.

2. Stand to the left of the person when you are serving food. If you are filling his glass, stand to his right. Avoid reaching directly in front of someone when serving him. Remove dishes from his right.

3. Try to keep the food at the right temperature. For faster service in a less formal setting, stand between two people and serve them at the same time.

4. Be careful not to bump or brush up against the guests as you move around them.

5. When you are serving food on a plate, hold the plate in your left hand, using your right hand to keep it level. As much as possible, keep your fingers from touching the top of the plate.

6. You may offer a second helping as guests begin to finish the main course.

7. Be sure everyone has finished each course before you start to remove the dishes. Remove the serving dishes first; then remove the guests' place settings. Do not stack dishes to carry them away. Leave the drinking glasses.

8. In less formal settings, you may remove two plates at a time and return with desserts for those two guests.

9. Refill drinks as you see they are empty, leaving the glasses in place if possible. A napkin under the pitcher can catch drips. If you are being served and do not want the drink, say "No, thank you" instead of turning your glass upside down, moving it, or holding your hand over it.

Thank the server when the meal is being served to you.

Night Out

Eating out can be an enjoyable experience for everyone. You may stop for dessert, have lunch with friends or family, or go to a fine restaurant for dinner. On any occasion where food is served away from home, there are specific guidelines.

1. Avoid going to a restaurant right before it closes. Make reservations if required.

2. Honor the dress code.

3. When you enter, wait to see if someone comes to seat you. If not, you may see a sign that indicates you should either wait to be seated or seat yourself.

4. If you have arrived before the others in your party, wait in the lobby.

    ◆ If members of your party have not arrived after a reasonable amount of time and you have been unable to contact them, you may leave the restaurant. Tip the waiter, however, for services he has rendered.
    ◆ If you arrive with another in your party, ask the waiter if you may be seated.
    ◆ Arrive early if you are the host. Show the first guest to your table and stay with him. Other guests will be shown to your table.

5. Seating:

    ◆ The lady follows the *maitre d'* (headwaiter) or hostess to the table, and the man follows her. The *maitre d'* pulls out the lady's chair for her.
    ◆ In a booth, the ladies sit on the inside and the gentlemen, on the outside.
    ◆ In a combination booth and table, guests sit in the booth, and the hosts sit in the chairs across from them. In the case of no special guests, ladies sit in the booth and gentlemen sit in the chairs.

WHEN YOU CLOSE THE MENU AND ARE READY TO ORDER

1. If someone asks you to dinner, he expects to pay. Do not arrive without money, however, in case there has been a misunderstanding. Order a moderately-priced meal. What the host says he will order should give you an idea as to the cost of the meal that you should order.

2. The person to the right of the host is the guest of honor and should be asked to order first.

3. Make your selection in a timely manner. Avoid changing your mind.

4. When ordering, say, "May I please have . . . ."

5. Quietly catch the waiter's attention by making eye contact with him or telling another waiter if necessary. Do not snap your fingers, tap a glass, call out, or get an item yourself. If someone is acting as host, he contacts the waiter for any service needed.

6. Thank the waiter when you are served.

7. It is not impolite to let the waiter know discreetly of any dissatisfactions with service or food early in the meal.

WHEN YOU ARE DINING

1. Do not draw undue attention to yourself.

2. Take what you need, but do not waste or play with the food or the seasonings.

3. If you are served food in a side dish, use the serving silverware to put the food onto your plate.

4. Do not play with sugar, packages of sweetener, silverware, or napkins. Do not write on the cloth or in the restrooms.

5. Dispose of wrappers, tea bag, etc. as neatly as possible. Try to place them all in one place such as on your bread and butter plate, service plate, saucer, or if nothing else is provided, under the rim of your dinner plate.

6. If a lady has excused herself and returns to the table, the gentlemen near her may slightly rise as she sits.

WHEN YOU HAVE FINISHED YOUR MEAL

1. Thank the waiter for the meal and ask him to give your compliments to the chef if you enjoyed the food.

2. Do not stack the dishes on the table to "help" the waiter. Do not hand the dishes to the waiter unless asked to do so.

3. As a courtesy to guests waiting for a table, to those waiting to bus (clear and reset) a table, and to waiters waiting to serve other customers, please leave in a reasonable time after the completion of the meal. If you are delayed for a longer period, increase your tip.

4. Never comb or put your hands in your hair when dining anywhere. Excuse yourself to the restroom for personal grooming. Keep your purse off the table.

5. After eating in a fast food restaurant, clear your table, return your tray to the proper place, clean up your paper and left over food, and throw away trash.

6. Paying the bill:

    • A very small group may ask for separate checks. In the case of a large group, it is best for one to pay the restaurant. Divide the amount of the bill equally unless some ordered much more or much less than others. Repay the person who paid the check.
    • The check may be brought on a tray to be paid at the table or paid at the cash register. If the host takes the check to the cashier, he may ask his guests to wait outside for him.
    • Be sure the bill is correct. Determine if the tip has been included before adding it. Make adjustments quietly.
    • The tip is 15% - 20% or more before taxes depending on extra services. It is appropriate to tip more if you have a large group. A 10% tip is appropriate for buffets.
    • Thank your host after he has paid the bill.

85

Thank You Notes

I Thessalonians 5:18

In every thing give thanks: for this is the will of God in Christ Jesus concerning you. King James Version

Give thanks in all circumstances, for this is God's will for you in Christ Jesus.   New International Version

Thank You Notes

Writing thank you notes gives you opportunities to let others know you appreciate their thoughtfulness. Others may have given of themselves through gifts, advice, visits, parties, condolences, help with homework or projects, hospitality, or by stepping in during a special time of need.

1. When expressing your thanks to someone, it is important to be prompt. Your timing is a further example of appreciation. If the thank you note is unavoidably delayed or if you forget to write, the note is better late than never.

2. When someone has made the effort to give a gift, he is encouraged when the gift is valued and remembered. Mention the gift again and how you have enjoyed it when you see the person.

3. If you receive a thank you note yourself, do not write a thank you note for the one you received. Take the opportunity, however, the next time you speak to the person to let her know you appreciated the nice note.

GUIDELINES FOR WRITING A THANK YOU NOTE

1. Start with *Dear*.

2. Name the gift. Do not mention the amount if the gift is money.

3. Tell what the gift means to you (where you will wear it, how you will spend the money, how much fun you had, how beneficial the help was). Never tell what might be wrong with a gift when you write your note.

4. Tell what the giving of the gift means to you.

5. Conclude your note with a parting remark and a closing such as "Love," "Much love," "Fondly," "God Bless You," or "Sincerely." Sign your name beneath the closing.

Example of a Thank You Note

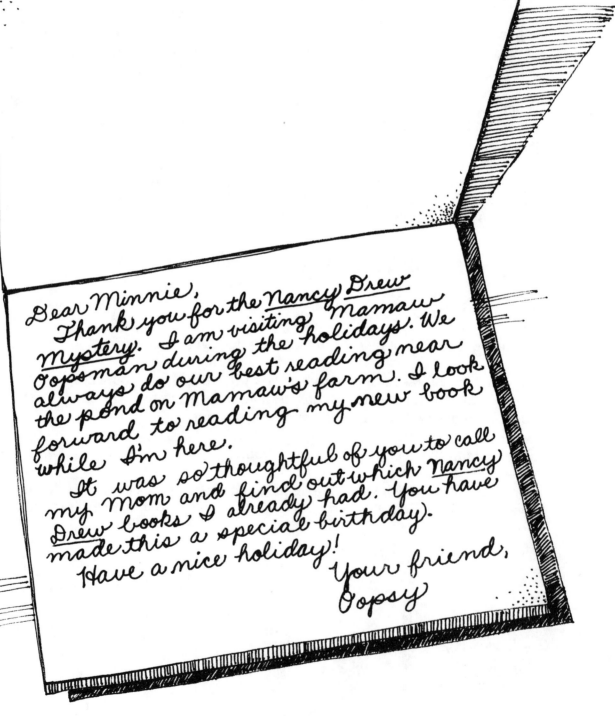

Dear Minnie,

Thank you for the <u>Nancy Drew Mystery</u>. I am visiting Mamaw Oopsman during the holidays. We always do our best reading near the pond on Mamaw's farm. I look forward to reading my new book while I'm here.

It was so thoughtful of you to call my Mom and find out which <u>Nancy Drew</u> books I already had. You have made this a special birthday. Have a nice holiday!

Your friend,
Oopsy

Oops, You're a Winner!

If you find yourself in a situation in which you are not sure what to say or do, use the following as guidelines:

1. Greet the other person.

2. Respect others' feelings, belongings, rules.

3. Try to make the situation pleasant.

4. Show appreciation.

5. Watch the hostess.

_____

You are always a winner when your good manners are showing!

Oopsdroppers
By Kymn

Oopsdropper One
met
Oopsdropper Two
and
found out together
what
Oopsdroppers
do.

They're silly little critters
That you'll hardly ever see - -
If you listen you won't hear them
And they're neither he nor she . . .

Oopsdropper One
and
Oopsdropper Two
picked a likely target
for what
Oopsdroppers
do.

A pretty little girl
Whose manners weren't that great - -
She didn't even remember
To say thank you or sit up straight!

With an
Oopsdropper laugh
and an
Oopsdropper smile
the
Oopsdroppers
dropped
in their usual style.

And this pretty little girl
With a fork in her hand
Quickly fell prey
To their Oopsdropped command.

While trying to remember
The manners she'd ignored
The food on her fork
Flew straight to the floor.

And the pretty little girl
With tears in her eyes
Said, "Oopsdroppers, Mommy,
They oopsdropped, that's why!"

And the
Oopsdroppers
giggled
as Oopsdroppers
do
cause other than children
believers are few.

The mother looked stern
With a mad-mommy face
And the Oopsdroppers
Oopsdropped right on out of that
place.

Now don't get feeling gloomy
If clumsy is your name - -
It might be the Oopsdroppers
Playing silly games.

That little girl realized
Soon after they departed
That Oopsdroppers oopsdrop
On poorly-mannered targets.

So . . . always mind your manners
And chances are you'll be protected
Cause those Oopsdroppers oopsdrop
When you very least expect it!

Set for Success

What I Have Learned about Table Settings

Getting Down to Basics

DINNERWARE

Use a matching set of dishes that are in good condition. (Use coordinating dishes if all pieces do not match.) The pattern on each plate should face the diner. Place the setting about an inch from the table's edge. Keep a service plate in place between courses at a formal dinner so that the place is never "empty." Place silverware evenly at each place setting. Place each setting evenly with the other settings at the table.

SILVERWARE

Only set the silverware that will be used during the meal, but always include the dinner fork, knife and spoon for balance. Use the same pattern of silverware if possible. If not, all forks and knives on the table should match, unless the knives have special handles. All spoons should match other spoons. Silverware brought in with other courses may have a different pattern.

NAPKIN AND BEVERAGE GLASS

Place the napkin on the plate, to the left of the fork, above the plate, or in the empty glass. Place the beverage glass on the right above the knife.

PLACE CARD

Use place cards or tell your guests where to sit. Do not set a place card for yourself. Place cards are especially helpful with more than eight guests. Place the cards above the setting, balance them on a napkin, or lean them on the glass if they are not folded. Place cards are most frequently used in formal settings.

Basic Setting

Figure 1   Place card above the plate, beverage glass above the knife, dinner fork, dinner plate with napkin, dinner knife (blade facing in), teaspoon.

Give Us Our Daily Bread

THE BREAD AND BUTTER PLATE

The bread and butter plate separates the bread from the juicy foods on the dinner plate. See Figure 3a on page 102 for placement. Place the bread on the side of the dinner plate if there is no other plate provided. In addition to bread and butter, the bread and butter plate may hold the butter knife, jelly, spoon for tea or coffee, a tea bag, finger foods or pits. Provide another plate if the meal produces many shells or bones, and place this plate above the bread and butter plate.

PASSING THE BREAD AND BUTTER

As bread is passed, take the piece closest to you. If you touch a piece of bread, you should take it. (This is true of any food.) If the loaf is uncut, the host slices or breaks a few pieces and then passes it for guests to slice or break pieces.

If a butter knife is passed with the butter, place it back with the butter after using it. If you accidentally put the butter knife on your plate, return it to the butter tray, if you can do so discreetly. Cut the butter from one end of the stick or tub, and place it on the side of your plate. If a seafood fork is passed with small sections of butter, use it to remove your pat of butter.

BUTTERING AND BREAKING THE BREAD

Put the bread on the plate and butter it there, or hold the bread slightly above the plate to butter it. Do not hold bread in the palm of your hand, on top of the table, or up in the air to butter it.

Break off small sections of bread with your hand (not your knife) and butter with the butter spreader. (Use your dinner knife for buttering bread if a spreader is not provided.) Eat the piece, butter the next piece and eat it. If the bread is served hot, butter all of it at once, but still break it in pieces to eat. This rule of etiquette is derived from the tradition that pieces of bread falling away from the plate or table were for the poor.

Use the dinner knife to butter your vegetables. You may use the butter spreader to butter corn on the cob. Except at the most formal dinners, you may place some bread into the gravy on your plate and eat the bread with your fork.

Beverages

COLD BEVERAGES

The beverage glass is set on the right above the knife. If additional glasses and cups are set, they are placed to the right of this glass. Hold your hand around a lemon or lime when squeezing the juice into the glass. The hostess should remove the seeds before serving the lemon. Avoid tapping on your glasses, playing with the straw, or crunching ice.

HOT BEVERAGES

Use a cup and saucer to serve coffee and hot tea. Turn the cup handle where it may be easily reached. See Figure 3b on page 103. The teaspoon is set on the saucer and returned to the saucer after use.

Place a tea bag in the teapot with hot water until the tea is strong enough, leaving the tag hanging outside the pot. When the tea is ready, use the spoon to press the tea bag against the side of the pot to release the excess liquid from the bag, and then place the bag on the saucer.

Protect the placemat or tablecloth from any used silverware. Place the teaspoon on a paper napkin, or place the bowl of the spoon down on your bread and butter plate or dinner plate.

Napkins or coasters should be accessible when beverages are served. If they are not, be careful where you set your drink. Moisture from the beverage may damage furniture.

97

Is It Soup Yet?

SOUP BOWL

Serve soup in a cup with one or two handles or in a bowl. Hold the cup by the handles if you choose to drink from it after spooning the first sips. Hold the spoon as you would hold a pencil, and skim the top of the soup to give it a chance to cool. Do not try to cool your soup by blowing on it or stirring it. If the soup in your mouth is too hot, take a drink of water. Do not spit soup out of your mouth. Unless there is danger of severe burning, do not spit any food out of your mouth.

SOUP SPOON

Sip from the end or side of the spoon. Do not put the entire spoon in your mouth unless the spoon is small. Do not put too much on your spoon; otherwise, you will slurp in an attempt to sip it all. As with any food, bring the silverware to your mouth and lean slightly forward. Spoon away from yourself to limit dripping and allow for cooling. When there is a small amount of soup left, tip the bowl away from yourself with one hand as you spoon the soup with the other hand.

A dinner plate or saucer should be placed under the soup bowl or cup. Place your soup spoon on the plate or saucer (to the right of the bowl) when it is not in use.

SOUP CRACKERS

You may place small crackers or croutons into your soup, a few at a time. Crumbling crackers into your soup looks messy.

Salad

SALAD PLATE

If the salad plate is on the dinner plate, eat the salad there. See Figure 2a below. If the salad plate is set to the left of the dinner plate, use your dinner fork to eat the salad there. See Figure 2b. If the salad plate is brought in after the main course, it replaces the dinner plate, and the salad should be eaten from where it is placed.

SALAD SILVERWARE

If a salad fork is provided, use it. Use the salad knife only if it is needed to cut the lettuce instead of folding the lettuce around the fork. Cutting the lettuce all at once, however, looks messy. Use the dinner knife if no salad knife is set.

When salad is served with the main course, no salad silverware should be set (Figure 2b). Use the dinner silverware.

SALAD BAR

When going to a salad bar, use the spoon or tongs provided. Do not use your fingers. Choose just what you will eat and go back later if necessary.

Figure 2a   Salad before dinner

Figure 2b   Salad with dinner

Napkins

The napkin should be in your lap before beginning the meal. If there is a napkin ring, remove it and lay it to the left above the plate. Wait for the hostess to place her napkin in her lap before placing yours. In a formal setting, also wait for the hostess to place her napkin on the table when she finishes. A waiter may place the napkin in your lap.

When placing a large napkin in your lap, fold it in half with the fold facing toward you. If the napkin is small, open it completely.

Use the napkin to: gently pat your mouth as needed.
clean your mouth before drinking.
clean something you spilled.
clean sticky fingers.
dry your hands in your lap after using a finger bowl.

Do not use your napkin to blow your nose or spit out food.

Keep the napkin in your lap until you are ready to leave the table. Then leave the napkin folded loosely to the left of the plate (or to the right if the hostess does) or in the center if the plate has been removed. Place your napkin in a manner to conceal a soiled area. Do not put a used napkin on the table during a meal. Place the napkin in your chair if you need to leave the table before you are finished eating.

A Five Course Meal

THE FIRST COURSE

The first course is the appetizer. If a seafood fork is set, you may be served shrimp cocktail, oysters on the half shell, snails (called escargot on a menu), or another seafood appetizer. The seafood fork is placed on the side that provides the most "balance" to the setting. See Figure 3a and Figure 3b on the next pages. If the seafood fork is set to the right of the spoon, it is either parallel to the spoon (Figure 3b) or with the tines resting on the bowl of the spoon.

THE SECOND COURSE

The soup spoon is for soup that will be served after the appetizer. Sometimes soup is the appetizer. The second course could be either soup or fish. If fish is served, a fish fork and fish knife may be set (Figure 3b).

THE THIRD COURSE

The third course is the entree (main course). Use the dinner knife and dinner fork (Figures 3a and 3b).

THE FOURTH COURSE

If several courses are served, salad may be served after the main course. The salad knife and fork are for the salad course (Figure 3a). Fruit and cheese may be served after, with, or in place of the salad. Instead of dessert, salad or fruit and cheese may be served. A cheese knife may be set when cheese is served.

THE FIFTH COURSE

The fifth course is the dessert. If it is a food that requires a fork and spoon, both will be placed at the top of the setting (Figure 3b) or brought with the dessert when it is served. The dessert silverware is not set in Figure 3a. A long teaspoon (for parfait or iced tea) is placed across the top of the place setting above the dessert spoon and in the same direction. In this case, the dessert fork is placed closest to the left of the plate or brought with the dessert.

Five Course Setting

Figure 3a   *Top Row*   Bread and butter plate with butter spreader, place card, beverage glass

Bottom Row Seafood fork, dinner fork, salad fork, dinner plate with napkin, salad knife, dinner knife, soup spoon

Note   When seated at a dinner with many courses, you may wonder which salad is yours and which water glass is yours. Simply remember that food dishes are on the left side of your setting and beverage glasses and cups are on the right side.

Figure 3b *Top Row* Salt and pepper shakers, dessert fork and spoon, beverage glass.

Bottom Row Napkin, fish fork, dinner fork, dinner plate, dinner knife, fish knife, soup spoon, seafood fork

Note A coffee cup, saucer, and spoon are often brought at the end of the meal.

Do not place more than three forks, three knives, or three spoons at a place setting. As exceptions to this rule, a seafood fork may be set to the right of the spoons and dessert silverware may be set above the plate.

103

Dinner Is Served

CUTTING FOOD

The American Style and the Continental Style are ways to use silverware during dinner. Choose the one most comfortable or the one used by those with whom you often dine.

In both styles, the fork begins in the left hand with the tines facing down into the food. Use the knife in your right hand to cut the food. With the Continental Style, continue holding the knife (or lay it on the top edge of your plate with the blade facing in). Keep the fork in your left hand with the tines still facing down as you eat. With the American Style, after cutting the food place the knife with the blade facing in, on the top edge of your plate. Take the fork (tines facing up) in your right hand, and eat the food from it.

Using either the Continental or the American Style, cut a few pieces at a time. If the meat is tough, try short cuts back and forth. Do not mix food together into a mess. Keep your elbows down as you cut, raising your arms up instead of out. Except in a formal setting, you may use the tip of your knife or your bread to push food onto your fork.

SILVERWARE DURING DINNER

Use the silverware farthest from each side of the dinner plate, and move toward the plate with each course. If you accidentally use the wrong silverware, keep using it throughout the course.

Do not motion with your hand while holding silverware. When you stop eating for a few moments or must excuse yourself from the table but will return, place your silverware in the resting position. See Figure 4 on the next page. This placement helps you avoid playing with your setting or with your food.

The waiter should not remove your plate when he sees your silverware in the position of Figure 4 on the next page.

AT MEAL'S END

Chew with your mouth closed and without unnecessary noises. Pace your eating so you finish at about the same time as everyone else. When you finish eating, position your silverware as shown in Figure 5 below. If food remains on your plate, move it aside before properly placing your silverware.

Leave your plate where it is instead of pushing it out of the way and saying you are finished or "stuffed" and could not eat another bite if someone paid you. Do not stack dishes at the table.

Sincerely thank the hostess. Offer to clean up. As a guest, do not leave the table until the hostess starts to leave, saying, "Let's go into the den" or "Shall we go into the living room?" At home, a child asks to be excused; an adult excuses himself. Push your chair in place as you leave.

Figure 4   Silverware Resting Postion

Figure 5   Silverware Finished Position

105

Finger Bowls and Dessert

FINGER BOWLS

Finger bowls are not common; however, when they are used, they are brought in near the end of the meal. The finger bowl (3/4 full of water) in Figure 6a (next page) is shown with a doily, a dessert plate, and silverware. Move the bowl and the doily to the left above the plate after cleaning your fingers. Place the silverware on the table beside the plate (See Figure 6b). If you have a fork but no spoon, place the fork to the right. The dessert silverware is larger than the salad silverware, however the salad silverware is often used.

If a napkin has been placed on top of the bowl, move it to the left beside the bowl. Dip your fingertips into the bowl (one hand at a time), carefully moving them through the water. Use the napkin to dry your fingers, returning it to the top of the bowl. If this napkin is not provided, use the napkin in your lap.

If no silverware is provided, keep the finger bowl in the center; there will be no more courses. If there is silverware but no water in the bowl, keep the bowl where it is; the dessert will be served in the bowl.

Do not use the water in the finger bowl to wipe your mouth. If a lemon is provided, rub it on your fingers.

DESSERT

Wait until the hostess begins eating her dessert before starting yours. Use either the spoon or the fork provided, leaving the other. The spoon is usually used for soft desserts and the fork for cakes and pies. To use both spoon and fork, use the fork to hold the food in place and the spoon to push or cut the food. A dessert containing fruit, for example, could require both fork and spoon. Coffee may be served during or after dessert.

SHARING DESSERT

Ask for an additional plate.

Use clean silverware to divide the food and place half on the additional plate, giving that to the other person.

Finger Bowl and Dessert Plate

Figure 6a   Finger bowl served on dessert plate

Figure 6b   Setting after finger bowl has been used

I'm Set for Success

Manners
to
Grow On

II Peter 3:18

But grow in grace, and in the knowledge of our Lord and Saviour Jesus Christ. To him be glory both now and for ever. Amen.   King James Version

Grow in the grace and knowledge of our Savior Jesus Christ. To him be glory both now and forever! Amen.   New International Version

Career Opportunities

When hiring employees, businesses seek those who take pride in their jobs, work well with others, and represent their companies favorably. The sooner you begin practicing good work habits and getting along with others, the more prepared you will be for successful career opportunities. Consider the following guidelines as you approach employment in the future.

THE RESUME

1. Try to use one page only.

2. Neatly type your resume on high quality paper, which will help your resume to stand out and give it a polished appearance.

3. Include information about your education, schools, degrees, studies, and achievements. List your experience with the most current employment first. Include positions as well as accomplishments. List activities that indicate experience or skill.

4. Consider those who may give you a reference. Contact them and request permission to include their names in your list of references. Then include "References available upon request" on your resume.

5. In your cover letter, briefly explain what you have to offer the company. Ask for an interview.

6. Let friends and acquaintances know that you are job hunting.

THE INTERVIEW

1. Dress neatly and conservatively. Look your best.

2. Be on time.

3. Stand until you are asked to be seated. Wait for the interviewer to complete other business. Have something of your own at which to look instead of looking through papers on his desk while you wait.

4. When the interviewer is ready for the interview to begin, look directly at him and make eye contact.

♦Sit up attentively.
♦Give direct answers.
♦Ask about the job and what your responsibilities would be.
♦Thank him for the interview.

5. If you are invited to dine out during an interview, remember your table manners.

6. Later, write the interviewer a thank you note. Express appreciation for his consideration, adding that you hope to hear from him soon.

7. Thank those who helped you get the interview or gave you a reference.

THE JOB

1. Be considerate of your boss and work within her system.

2. If you must question your boss' decisions, do so privately. Do not speak critically of her or of the company.

3. Keep the boss informed of your work and progress. Keep good records.

4. Be friendly and respectful to everyone. Do not get involved in office gossip. Be helpful.

5. When anyone enters your office for the first time that day, rise and offer a seat.

6. Keep your desk or work area clean.

7. Use your time well. Use extra time to the benefit of the company.

8. When in leadership, take charge without being "pushy."

THE TIME TO LEAVE

1. Leave on the best terms possible with management and fellow employees. The relationships you have formed, memories you will have, and future references you will need are far more important than your openly venting any frustrations.

2. Do a good job until you leave. It is your fellow employees who will need to fulfill any responsibilities left undone.

3. You may later enjoy paying a brief visit to your former company. Be careful not to interfere with work.

Weddings

You will attend more and more weddings as your friends are married and you are asked to be in weddings. A wedding is an important occasion. Friends and family should be supportive in attending.

Take the opportunity to get ideas for your own wedding. Businesses that specialize in invitations, cakes, attire, and flowers should be able to give valuable advice. Do not hesitate to consult wedding etiquette books when you are ready for your own special day even when you are planning a small wedding or when you are in a wedding party.

SPECIAL EVENTS BEFORE THE WEDDING

During the planning of a wedding, special parties may be given, including engagement parties, bridal showers, brunches, luncheons, dinners, formal and informal celebrations.

GIFT GIVING

Give a gift if you are invited and choose to attend the wedding. You may want to give a gift even if you do not attend the wedding. The wedding gift is separate from a shower gift.

Many couples register requests at a store, where a clerk may assist you in making a selection. Arrange for the store to send the gift or deliver it yourself before the wedding day. It is inconvenient for the family if gifts are brought to the reception. Gifts may be sent later if necessary. If the wedding is canceled, do not ask for your gift back, but all gifts should be returned.

WHAT TO WEAR

What you wear should be appropriate for the season and the time of day that the wedding is set. Always remember you are not there to outshine the bride and groom. Do not wear white.

WHERE TO SIT

The usher leads you to your seat. Usually the bride's family and friends are seated on the left side and the groom's on the right, unless the numbers are exceptionally uneven. If you arrive early, you may take an aisle seat on the appropriate side. Talk quietly with other guests. Do not, however, move around visiting or changing seats.

The grandmothers are escorted to seats at the front; their husbands follow. The groom's mother is then escorted to her seat at the front as her husband follows. The bride's mother is seated last. The attendants enter and proceed to the front. Traditionally, the bride's mother stands to watch the bride as she enters. At this time, all guests stand, facing the bride as she proceeds to the front. The ceremony begins, and the guests take their seats. When the wedding is over, leave your seat after the parents and grandparents leave.

AFTER THE WEDDING

Following the wedding ceremony, pictures are often taken of the bridal party; you may be invited to watch or to proceed to a reception. There may be a receiving line at the reception. In the line will be the bride's mother (hostess), groom's mother, the bride, the groom, maid or matron of honor, and the bridesmaids who may take their places at the end. The fathers may take their places beside their wives.

When going through the line, introduce yourself to the bride's mother. She may introduce you to the next in line, or introduce yourself if she does not. Tell the parents how lovely the wedding was and perhaps how you know the couple. Tell the bride how beautiful she is and congratulate the couple. Say hello to the bridesmaids. Be brief and pleasant, remembering that many others will want to go through the line. Do not go through the line with food or drink in your hands.

As a guest at a wedding, you should be able to introduce yourself to other guests and discuss the couple and the wedding. Gather around the wedding cake when the couple is ready to cut it. The cutting of the cake is a special part of the reception, and showing your interest may encourage others to do so.

WHEN THE RECEPTION IS OVER

After the bride throws the bouquet, the couple is usually ready to leave. Traditionally rice, birdseed, or something similar is provided and thrown on the couple as they leave. The reception has ended at this time, and all guests should proceed to leave.

A note or telephone call after the wedding to the mother of the bride is a nice gesture to let her know how much you enjoyed the wedding and that you were delighted to be a part of celebrating the event.

Hospital Visits

WHEN YOU ARE THE PATIENT . . .

Being sick can be overwhelming. Concentrate on your healing and taking care of your needs; for instance, excuse yourself to eat, if visitors are present. Introduce visitors to others only if you feel well enough.

WHEN YOU LEAVE THE HOSPITAL . . .

1. You may tip the clean up attendant a few dollars and give a gift for the nurses to share or give small gifts to a few nurses who were especially helpful.

2. You may leave your flowers for others in the hospital.

3. Write thank you notes for all calls, cards, visits and gifts.

YOU CAN HELP THE PATIENT WHEN YOU . . .

1. Bring a gift of flowers, magazines or books of interest to her, stationery and stamps, or music. If the hospital stay is long, a new gown or robe may be useful.

2. Ask if you could get something for her before you leave.

3. Offer to help at the patient's home by picking up the mail, feeding the dog, baby-sitting, or preparing meals for the family. When delivering meals use disposable dishes if possible, to relieve the person from having to return dishes or containers. Prepare a basket with a variety of snacks, mints, fruits, devotional books, magazines, toothpaste and a new toothbrush for out of town guests or family staying with the patient.

4. Ask if you may offer a prayer for improved health and skill for the doctors.

5. Call and send cards.

6. Visit a short period and look for signs of her tiring.

7. Ask how she is feeling and do not press for details of the illness.

   ◆Keep the conversation light. This is not the time to bring up anything negative about which she does not need to know.
   ◆There is no need to compare your own illness to hers.
   ◆Keep your voice down, and do not carry on a lot of conversation with others in the room.

Funeral Services

A funeral is a time of great sensitivity and sorrow. You may attend because you have lost someone close to you or you are showing your love and concern for a friend. There are a few things to know that will help you in either case.

1. Wear conservative clothes.

2. Choose a topic of conversation which helps to express your sympathy and sensitivity during this time.

    ◆ Do not ask for details about the death.
    ◆ Say you are sorry, you will miss him, he was very special to you.
    ◆ Families may be comforted by hearing such things as how many people are in attendance and how beautiful the church looks.
    ◆ You may bring up other general subjects.
    ◆ You may smile but should avoid laughing.
    ◆ The family should thank you for coming and send thank you notes for all condolences.

3. Sit between the middle and the back of the church. The family and/or pall bearers sit at the front.

4. You may send a note of condolence even if you see the family.

5. Help the grieving family in the best way you can. Take food to the family. Include paper products, drinks, mints, and hand lotion. You also may offer to pick up family from the airport, stay at the house to receive food, or help with the laundry. You may send flowers to the funeral home or make a contribution to a charity that was of special interest.

6. Be attentive to the family after some time has passed. Several weeks after the funeral could be the hardest time.

Good Manners Report Cards